Patience, Therefore

# OTHER WORK BY DARIL BENTLEY

## POETRY

*In That Other Life*
*A Shanty Kingdom*
*The Long Lake*
*Certain Mercies*
*Minding Silence*
*The Vinedressers*
*The Box*

## REFERENCE

*The Bentley Guide to Poets & Poetry
in English: Chaucer to Brodsky*

# Patience, Therefore

*Verses Toward Calm amid Chaos*

DARIL BENTLEY

RESOURCE *Publications* · Eugene, Oregon

PATIENCE, THEREFORE
Verses Toward Calm amid Chaos

Copyright © 2022 Daril Bentley. All rights reserved. Except for brief quotations in critical publications or reviews, no part of this book may be reproduced in any manner without prior written permission from the publisher. Write: Permissions, Wipf and Stock Publishers, 199 W. 8th Ave., Suite 3, Eugene, OR 97401.

Resource Publications
An Imprint of Wipf and Stock Publishers
199 W. 8th Ave., Suite 3
Eugene, OR 97401

www.wipfandstock.com

PAPERBACK ISBN: 978-1-6667-5397-4
HARDCOVER ISBN: 978-1-6667-5398-1
EBOOK ISBN: 978-1-6667-5399-8

10/04/22

For David James

# CONTENTS

*Acknowledgments*     xi
*Author's Statement*     xiii

## I | THE LESSONS OF CHAOS

| | |
|---|---|
| Rumor Has It | 3 |
| Harsh Harvest | 4 |
| Winnowing the Fields | 5 |
| Sol on Stone and Water | 6 |
| The Idle Magi | 7 |
| Calf Found in a Field in the Rain | 8 |
| Three-page Liturgy | 9 |
| Remnant Barnyard | 10 |
| These Were Children | 11 |
| Words of a Pebble | 12 |
| Lady of the Evening | 13 |
| The Mad Cascade | 14 |
| Large Lawns | 16 |
| Rush Hour | 17 |
| Laundromat | 18 |
| Saving the World | 20 |
| World Over | 21 |
| Domed Silos | 22 |
| Archimedes' Screw | 23 |
| Satan Strolls the South Side | 24 |
| A Note for Keats' Ode | 25 |
| The Bigger Deals | 26 |
| Hydrant | 28 |
| Judgment Seat | 29 |
| These New Pharisees | 30 |
| Hydra Over Haiti | 31 |

CONTENTS

Roadside Artifacts 32
Specter Near a Church 33
Hymn for Sixty-eight 34
The Mendicants of 49th Street 36
Rimas Dissolutas Corvus 37
The Red Clock 38

## II | A PROMISE OF SOLACE

Black Hole 41
Ten Million Moons 42
Crescent Moon 43
John Paul II 44
Around Troupsburg 45
Watching Amish Farmers 46
Field Hands 47
Tour of the Big Apple 48
Vesper 49
The Fence Line 50
Sonnet for a Primal Wood 51
Let These Consecrate May 52
Three Apple Trees Seen as if Cast in Bronze 53
Burdock 54
I Dreamt of Fawns 55
A Supplication 56
A Distant Wood 57
Saguaro 58
Wind in a Wood 59
Girl with Milkweed 60
Ball Gone Astray 61
Aspens Reflected on Water 62
Retreat for an Amputee 63
The Fall 64

## CONTENTS

| | |
|---|---|
| Missive for the Realtor | 65 |
| Coin for a Friend, Violated | 66 |
| An Old Southerner Responds to a Train | 67 |
| Spiders' Threads | 68 |
| Selective Memory | 69 |
| John Conrad | 70 |
| Suburban Ritual | 71 |
| Moonlit Private Drive | 72 |
| The Martyrs | 73 |
| All My Bones | 74 |
| Michelangelo | 75 |
| Granite Proclamations | 76 |
| Leaf and Afterlife | 77 |
| Winter Depths | 78 |
| Fountainhead | 79 |
| Palm Reading | 80 |
| *About the Author* | 81 |

# ACKNOWLEDGMENTS

Grateful acknowledgment is made to the following for original publication and reservation of copyright and publication rights to the author.

"All My Bones" (*The Lyric*)
"An Old Southerner Responds to a Train" (*Irvine Burns Club Broadside*)
"Archimedes' Screw" (*The Chained Muse*)
"Aspens Reflected on Water" (*CircleShow*)
"Ball Gone Astray" (*Better Than Starbucks*)
"Black Hole" (*Boing Boing*)
"Burdock" (*CircleShow*)
"Coin for a Friend, Violated" (*Irvine Burns Club Broadside*)
"Laundromat" (*Fine Madness*)
"Let These Consecrate May" (*The Avocet*)
"Michelangelo" (*The Chained Muse*)
"Missive for the Realtor" (*Delyow Derow*)
"Retreat for an Amputee" (*The Avocet*)
"Rimas Dissolutas Corvus" (*Words on Walls*)
"Roadside Artifacts" (*CircleShow*)
"Rumor Has It" (*Blue Unicorn*)
"Saguaro" (*The 64 Best Poets of 2018*, Black Mountain Press)
"The Fall" (*Time of Singing*)
"The Mad Cascade" (*The 64 Best Poets of 2018*, Black Mountain Press)
"The Mendicants of 49th Street" (*Clutch*)
"Three Apple Trees Seen as if Cast in Bronze" (*The Avocet*)
"Winter Depths" (*Journal of the Isles*)

## AUTHOR'S STATEMENT

The author of this work is a Christian first and a poet second, if he is indeed worthy of either title. He was raised to observe the good and to shun what is not. The author begs forgiveness for any offense taken from the words or sentiments of this work—conveyed from an honest heart, if not from the humility of a judicious tongue.

"Be patient therefore, brethren,
unto the coming of the Lord."

—James 5:7 (KJV)

# I

# The Lessons of Chaos

# RUMOR HAS IT

And there will be wars and rumors
of inherited wars—

And the next administration
will not send its only son

But will rely on yours.
And still the peace will not be won.

# HARSH HARVEST

An oat field rolled like a lake
of rippling green
my hands swam through

When my supple
fingers were not yet ready
for the scythe.

Give that relic of a tool to me.
I'm prepared to
bring down half this ample

Recent Edom I've seen
overrun with tares
and their harvest of wars.

And the limbs were lithe
that having grown older ache
a reaper's remedy.

# WINNOWING THE FIELDS

In spring rains farmers sow—
and through the spring and summer under
cathedral sunlight sown grains grow.

And then fields ripen to brown—
and the cowl brown of autumn's stained-glass torpor
in an instant is cut down.

The grain is winnowed of its chaff—
and the chaff goes with the wind,
and the wind and the winnowing laugh

To see our children off to war.
The flails and baskets have uncounted harvests sinned—
and still the winds of winters howl for more.

# SOL ON STONE AND WATER

"The way we are with one another should establish a temple.
Not the temple sand and lever build
but whatever's made and maintained
as the indivisible waters flow.

But we do not envision or keep it so,"
says my friend Solomon, a mason of considerable skill.
"The water teaches us how peaceably we should go
upon this rock, but that is never sustained.

That is not the way we have been—
not how our lives have been wrought with the tools we wield.
The stone splits wrong and rain delays the project.
We become deaf to ebb and flow and dumb

Of tongue, hard and impermeable.
What does it cost to offer a hand despite the fact
that the foundation is strained
and the mortar sets up rather slow.

Like stones or bricks the seemingly insignificant act
is what builds the wall—and the wall
holds up the house in which we all must live awhile
with others before we all must go."

So my good and wise friend Solomon Holds-the-Sky has held,
who argues that fire and flood will come
and our brethren will listen
only when this heated globe has cracked.

# THE IDLE MAGI

In a farmyard out in just about anywhere
three antique tractors gather dust
from the secondary road that runs nearby.

Just what they have sat here waiting for
for so long is up in the air.
Their purpose seems without much sense

To keep the vigil of a rust
from spring to summer to autumn sky.
I make of them brothers gathered to confer—

Three magi almost lost
but guided by a moon and a star
on some path of greatest consequence.

They consult the heavens until morning.
In perfect silence they listen, as they must,
to a great horned owl's emphatic warning.

They sit at angles to one another's mind,
knowing now just where they are
for recalling just where they were

When told to carry forth the cost
of working an earth worth not much more
than mud on the boots of humankind.

# CALF FOUND IN A FIELD IN THE RAIN

*There* you are—your mother standing lost beside you.
She has given up licking you back to life.
>She just makes a helpless moan of appeal.

I can do nothing for her but stroke her baffled neck.
Noah worked God's will in all kinds of weather.
>And once more the land offered bondage.

Do they do life and death better in other solar systems?
There's no apparent reason you should have died—
>except whatever explanation might radiate

From the dark, cosmic center of your lifeless eye.
Of course it is raining. It ought to pummel down
>in a deluge and wash away this hard world.

# THREE-PAGE LITURGY

A leaf is wandering here and there,
directionless on the wind
and subject to an indifferent air.

Another is cartwheeling
over the lawn; vain, unable to find
its purpose in the world.

A third is languishing, caught
as if crucified dry and dying curled
on a rose bush thorn.

I realize I have been taught
three reasons to be kneeling
before a certain tree since I was born.

# REMNANT BARNYARD

The wild clematis is arguing its ascent through stones
and up the mossy bark
of a decrepit maple time ill affords,
and a fussy-old populist hinge complains

Of these weak boards in barn and silo
that settle their creaky bones
in the leer-eyed straw-dust dinge of the day.

The tin rooster listens patiently clutched atop its arrow
in the rusty skyline dim
to the contentious conversations
offered by the wind.

I want to tell the seasonal laborers to fashion of these
the beauties of absent overlords.
I want to say to them hurry, it will soon be dark

And there is promise of rain and with most of the hay
not in. I recommend
the unforgiving action at the rim
of this cranky pump-well handle. Tomorrow,

I may not come here again—what with other duties.
But someone should know
where the byway stands of sanity have been abandoned.

# THESE WERE CHILDREN

These were children
once one in Nemean lion's-hide coveralls
    with the dust and the mud—

Playing at Herculean tasks
until young limbs and heads in sunlit halls
    were hero bronzed.

Their supple skin
beneath prided pelts could be washed then
    with simple soap

To a bubble-buffed and glorious glow.
These waifs shed their masks
    and went to work in Augean stalls—

And covered in
the dust of knowledge and in carnal crud
    relinquished hope

And took on for wages the filth of men
that cannot somehow even now be cleansed
    of what men know.

# WORDS OF A PEBBLE

What do the leaves speak of
when they assemble in clattering conclave?
And when they are chattering,

Do they all talk of the same thing
or are they engaged in many conversations?
Do they care a whit what a human knows?

Is it freedom or conquest they crave?
How do they define, "to live"?
And what does a pebble inquire of another

Kicked down a path by the blind
toes of our foot-in-mouth perambulations?
Does it chide?—"He is representative

Of these armed beings that purport to love.
If I were human, I'd be stepping rather
carefully so as to choose my destinations

With the cares of lesser things in mind.
And I'd want to know if trees keep track of
where and to whom the loose leaf goes."

# LADY OF THE EVENING

She tells her story to a common John
because, why not.
He's a nice guy and has time and she

Isn't for a change
being badgered and abused
by a pimp.

She was, to be specific, born in Bonn,
Germany.
She was a military brat who got

Tired of globetrotting and decided to,
so to speak, "run away from home."
She was hungry.

She was too young to work legally.
Life and its many needs can disarrange.
She doesn't have to purchase used.

Now she can buy all brand new.
"I take care of that old man on Brome,
too," she says. "He's a gimp."

# THE MAD CASCADE

So we are not these leaves
that imbibe the sun,
that apprehend its giving
and run

With it along the vein
to inflate the lung—
and briefly breathe in awe
of incorporeal kind.

And slowly accrue
a body in which the living
of the sun is done.
So we grasp for branch

That is not there
as we're covered by Time
the avalanche.
We climb

Miniscule hills of mystery
in the hollow we've made
to hide in air
the mad cascade

Of human history.
So we've not the lives we
had in mind.
Spread thin

Along a faithless chain,
the meaning groans within
a cyclic thaw—
weakened reasons clung

Tenuously to
cliffs of earthly lives.
The end was breath begun—
the leggy life of humanity

Standing at the margin
of a mountain
ready to fulfill the law
of a lofty shroud down-flung.

# LARGE LAWNS

The good chur-
chgoers
 will,

Idling tomorrow
 and cur-
sing the national

News
 and Saturday
mowers

That haltingly go,
 still
in plush pews

Wor-
ship what they
 mow.

# RUSH HOUR

Car after car,
every motor hurries—
for where
it does not know.

Every martyr worries
they are not there—
but *there*, so far,
is but a tentative tease

Of stripes on tar.
And so,
clueless as to where
the striping leads—

Horn and glare,
*Christ* in their screeds,
from where they are
they go.

# LAUNDROMAT

In the fogbound porthole
    of the drier,
clothes tumble about
like promises, like
treaties, like delegates
gone haywire.
                Now

A shirt comes around again
    like a limp
handshake
bonding covenants
                of doubt.
    A pact is struck

Between fitted
    and top
sheets out of their entente
cordiale.
And in the mix
                one's own
    resolutions: a sock

Without companion;
an earnest pair
                of pants,
legs akimbo,
inside-out, unable to meet;
    underwear

Fated for some other rôle;
an almost-discernible
                    logo,
like life's misplaced stamp
of approval of a quick fix.
    These are shipmates
of the threadbare towel,

Emissary of détente,
relaying dog-eared charter
sent, sent back, and remitted
    again and again—
like an ineffectual, effete
        vow.

# SAVING THE WORLD

Chechnya and the Ukraine. Fire. Flood. Hurricane.
Tunisia and Lebanon. Israel. Gaza Strip. Pakistan.
      Egypt. Syria.
Iraq. Iran. Rape. Rioting. Genocide. Embassy attack.
Indonesia. Taiwan. Earthquake and volcano.
      Afghanistan.

New York and Chicago. Detroit. Philadelphia.
Tsunami and landslide. Arizona. Texas. California.
      New Mexico.
Africa. South America. Mayhem. Persecution.
Bangladesh. Somalia. Hatred. Oppression. Cyclone.
      Typhoon. Darfur.

Miami. L.A. War. Pestilence. Famine. Corruption.
of persons and places, as ever—wherever
      humans go.
I retrieve the black glove the elderly woman
has dropped on the snowy avenue and hand it back
      demurely to her.

# WORLD OVER

Over and over
a world rolls stone
away from tomb,
from broken bone.

By night, by day—
all the world over
a love roams lone,
a hate spells doom.

The poor forever
make their way
with wail and moan.
Again and again

The world is womb
and seed of men
that make us pay
for limb—for lover.

# DOMED SILOS

The silos we do not like to think about
stop where the ground begins.
They are hidden by the Need to Know
we impose upon our subterranean better angels—

The crosses on church spires a counterweight
to Armageddon.
It does not matter if it's Sonora Desert

Or High Plains or Appalachian dells
of reasonable doubt
that militaries make a show of self-control
at the bending of the bow.

So, too, the bullet is created round and straight.
The most romantic ones
are capped in red or silver or gold.

You see them in Eugene Oregon
and Blue Springs Kansas lands of chert
and Louisiana ranchland sold
to Pennsylvania's bags of coal.

And here's a green one,
and here's a blue, to house those clouds that go
toward the wintering of heavens and hells.

# ARCHIMEDES' SCREW

Archimedes could not draw water from stone,
but with his screw
could make it run uphill.
The splendid turn of a fluid mind,
his pulleys dashed Marcellus' crew

Upon the rocks of Syracuse.
Being by nature placid, kind,
he did not much condone
the employ of force yet applied it rather well
to defend against or kill

The armies of the Roman noose.
In fact, Archimedes soon grew
as dispossessed of as bored
with warring by recourse to intellectual skill.
When a soldier slew

Him at point of sword,
he graciously left his body behind
by turning and offering up at will
his rarefied defenses to be other-army scored
against the legions of another hell.

# SATAN STROLLS THE SOUTH SIDE

I chose that rock that Eve's son lifted.
I clad the calf that Aaron made.
I lined the Queen of Sheba's sandals.
I provided Pontius Pilate's shade.

I chewed the strings of the purse
brave Judas hefted.
You'd not imagine just what I'm worth.

I fashioned Mengele-forceps twisted.
I put the bullets in your pistols.
I drive-by to and fro about your earth.
I carved the keystone set in Babel's

Tower. I was laugh-
ter first at Adam's curse.
Crack & cut of sidewalk serve my staff.

# A NOTE FOR KEATS' ODE

Perhaps even the cosmic crockery can split.
It was written that Lucifer seeking to reduce the stars
a third looked into it.

The infamous urn of truth and beauty is ever ours
to justify to posterity its classical handles suspended
from its purposes quit.

Some say some rifts can't be mended.
And some defend the daystar cracked and busted jars
of cultures self-ended.

Call him Enemy of Amphora. Did he gaze into the pit
of the bottomless vessels of humanity's endless wars
and the lids offended?

# THE BIGGER DEALS

The bigger deals slouch
around a table
and place their bets.
They've already won
everything they've wanted.
The bigger deals control
the law
and the water and
the air. The bigger deals
say when
and say how high.
They could cure the ills
of the city, but
what profit is in that?
The bigger deals are made
in a soundproof room
on an island
of material degradation.
Latitude: They are.
Longitude: They will.
The bigger deals own
poverty
and injustice.
These mere trifles hang
upon their walls.
They make jokes about
the one percent
as pretenders to the game.
The bigger deals push
stacks of plastic nations

to the middle of the felt.
Their anecdotes
of loss and gain
run to relative accounts
of wealth and power.
The bigger deals wear
opportunity like watches
with diamond works
and platinum surrounds.
They've divided time
in roughly equal measure
among themselves.
Philanthropy is a top hat
they wear to Royal Ascot.
Their horses never lose.
Their flowers never wilt.
They use technology
envied by demonic worlds.
They place wagers
on live refugee outcomes.
The bigger deals run K
Street & 5th Ave. An under-
weight child saved is a tax
write-off by which
they underwrite large lies.

# HYDRANT

Not Xinjiang nor Altar. Not Kosovo.
                       The bodies ran.
The bodies leaped and twisted
and fell as they would—
                       water just to have.

Not under gaze of Hydra but Pan.
                       Children. Not man.
The bodies giggled.
The bodies laughed. A body's blood
                       rose in exultation.

The bodies passed through
                       a rainbow of sun
touching the arcs of cool come
to the corner of a block where
                       revived with water

Pooled the offspring of the poor.
                       The bodies bled
relief from heat and boredom.
Not Aleppo.
                       Not Juba. Not Kiev.

# JUDGMENT SEAT

This dying man I sit beside
and watch breathe roughly
in a bed in a hospital is buried
in snow—pillow
a wind-drift crusty cap to kill
the cold reality of the frosty hair
that's lain upon his head.

This is not a Christmas father.
And this is not his visage old—
with its sunken cheek
and carven wrinkle. No holly
wreathe frames face so pallid.
This is not the weather
from his Sun Belt retirement

Community lately reported. This
is skin into which the dying go.
Where is the sunlight in me
willing to empurple the pallor
upon an eyelid? Is it
for me a child to deem it good
or ill he made this make of bed?

# THESE NEW PHARISEES

Quoters of scripture for sport
and profit, dunners
of the wayward poor, and in short

Salvation's lottery winners
of entrepreneurial wiles:
They've made of the Savior their

Reclusive cult,
bleeding him of forbear-
ance and clemency to a fiscal fault—

Not to be dispensed
to steel the mortal mettle
against temptation and weakness

But spirited away with the saved
to be licensed
with the blood they peddle

As self-sanctimonious
red-dyed tap water in holy phials
with matching retail silver cups.

Pray. Pray, lest three precious drops
of God's marketable love be laved
upon losers and sinners.

# HYDRA OVER HAITI

If you connected
the countless dots
of Hydra tail to head to head to head

And pulled them down
as if the catch
of island fishermen—

To feed the poor
would still require
untold galaxies of net-mending space

And lots and lots
of spools of light for
gapping thread.

And still the alien poor would drown.
And still in darkness
the Dragon's fire

Would scorch
the water as if it had not been
that seas would cool to touch His face.

# ROADSIDE ARTIFACTS

I confess I have a time or two along the road
collected from the cinders the bottle caps
and plastic soldiers and the metal washers and wing nuts

That scattered like bizarre blessings secure
I don't know what.
And more than once—

Nailed with the red-bandana caution rags of alienation
to protruding lumber passing the dented
and fender-scraped guard rails of defiance,

And weary (deathly weary) of the petty fine points argued
by miscreants on either side
of ephemeral fixations—

I have smoked from fortune's
unholy reliquary this filthy, crumpled, secondary-highway
fag; this suspect cigarette butt.

# SPECTER NEAR A CHURCH

Blessed with a tongue acutely duplicitous,
he has sold them many lies from his
well-articulated portmanteau of tortured biblical verses.
He clutches a fist-

ful of nickels that are all
ever his lips have kissed with a tenderness.
He knows in the lexical recesses of his lascivious loins
that he is winning

In the morphemes and sanctuaries of the mortal.
He spits. He curses
as he rubs the coins
a good long time together.

He belches. He twists his head up toward an ashen mist
portending ill weather
mirrored in the pit of pernicious eyes—
and he is grinning.

# HYMN FOR SIXTY-EIGHT

You couldn't ignore 1968. You couldn't pretend, like one
tries to do with the pandemic 2020s, that it just didn't happen.
LBJ in the White House hostage to war escalation
and the prospect of defeat.
Nixon in an electoral wipeout of Humphrey.
Wallace with more votes than should have been.
Wallace (pre-Trump) with an alarming following of robots.
Wallace with more power than should have been.
Wallace with more dogs than peaceful protesters on the street.
The handlers should have gone to Hades

Just for turning those innocent dogs into raging canine bigots.
Wallace nostalgic for plenty of hoses.
It was for their own good. Separate but equal—
except that separate was cool but equal was not.
"Is this us?" one said, even at the untutored age of nine.
Thank heavens for enlightened parents.
If we didn't mind our manners at our black friends' houses
we were in trouble—
and no one listened to the neighbors who clicked their tongues
as they withdrew inside, commenting on the shame of it all.

What perpetual color-coded land was the country aspiring to?
Mr. Jones, who had the Punch-and-Judy show,
later gave me my first job.
I painted his house, and I was proud of it.
I don't know if pride was merited, but if it wasn't Mr. Jones
never said anything. He knew a little about intolerance.
They didn't teach history right in school.
They taught us about the institution of slavery
and the antebellum south and Jim Crow
but the textbooks never ventured explicit images of lynchings.

What would Punch and Judy think of that?
How would Mrs. Prim of the school board carry her slim bones
past the lunch lady?
The operative word that year was *turmoil*.
The country was morphing into something like a blue
funk and crisis about what it was—thrown together in a mob
painting by LeRoy Neiman psychedelic with riots, and free love,
and Viet Nam War demonstration, and the wrack
and convulsion of unrest, and fears, and questionings,
and the precarious thrust and balance of civil rights legislation.

In the melee this calm black man began to softly sound
his heart and people went silent and the only thing heard otherwise
from the crowd was a rhythmic "Amen"
to words only he seemed to have learned the meaning of.
Something more powerful than hatred began to attack
Theophilus Eugene "Bull" Connor and the kings
of the still-remaining Enslavement Forever underground.
With a holy imprimatur, he took their measure to reduce their size.
This man carried himself as if he saw something beyond
the warhorses of the marble and granite gentlemen.

I was a child, innocent enough not to be fooled. He was like
the Bible prophets Grandmother Mary was so fond of.
Except that this man was a real-life magus, a druid, a faith-seer.
He needed no brain-bashing baton or spell-casting wand.
He needed no bulwark of jackboot glories.
He was there on TV—and when the camera zoomed in
and you could see his eyes you thought about the sadness there
like in Lincoln's eyes deeper and more profound
even than Great Grandmother's stories
of when in County Cavan, Ireland, all the potatoes had turned black.

# THE MENDICANTS OF 49TH STREET

The unmedicated—I do not know if fed—homeless man
is walking around and around a honey locust
newly planted here on 49th Street, Manhattan,

Feverishly muttering to some other self the gist of a quest
or reminiscence only he
knows the significance of. And so I am slowly chasing

Him, invoking grace of his angels that if we persist
he and I might someday emerge somewhere
in this life anywhere near a conclusion on an ambition

Or a bit of luck to be milked or a love affair
or the legacy of a friendless journey
through this unimaginable wilderness worthy of retracing.

# RIMAS DISSOLUTAS CORVUS

These crows,
opportunistic March pickets,
laze on winter's lovely withered branches

In legions getting by
on stark, cold caws—
centurion to some death-and-carrion duty.

These bros
in their livid leather jackets
idle the Ides away on weathered benches,

Daring passersby
to utter outworn laws—
sentry to a belligerent and forsaken beauty.

# THE RED CLOCK

A red clock hangs
    in the archives of men
filled with their pages
    of murderous crime.

The clock is red
with the blood of the ages
by tribes spilled—by gangs
    at havoc and war

For churches and kingdoms.
    The clock keeps time
as the passage of gore
    and mayhem is written.

When the end of all comes,
the red clock will chime
for the innocent dead
    and the massacred poor.

# II

# A Promise of Solace

# BLACK HOLE

Lies within ourselves a star burned out—
in ourselves, a blinding glory.
Pick this rock or any other
to burn upon a doubt

The image of one's brother
to tell this dismal tale or any other story.
Vies within us expanding star

With, within ourselves, a gravity dark.
Place all planets one to another,
they could not pull in who we are
or circumscribe the awful arc

Of time and its human quarry
through a universe moot in much about
how near love is or far.

# TEN MILLION MOONS

When the white light of the moon
among a congregation of ten
million moons

Rests upon the lawn and drifts
into my darkened rooms,
I lean at the door—

Pondering among a host of dooms
that can occur to men
why peace should not as soon

As strife grace earthly floor
among the infinite unions and rifts
of ten million soons.

# CRESCENT MOON

Looking up where stars are hewn
into an ebony height,
I seem to recall from I don't know when

This silver seed strewn
across a black-slate millhouse floor—
with an ivory-bladed sickle hung

On a nail beside an ancient granary door
that opens now and then
to reveal a widening wedge of light

Dispersed across this field of men,
who gather in at night
against their fears their wondering young.

# JOHN PAUL II

Perhaps the best of the gifts of his soul
was a poem he wrote
about a splendid golden-swaying wall
of wheat beneath the sun

And of scythes cutting
with soft and somber sound
in unhurried, all-encompassing motion.

We are as the wheat
threshed by shafts of daylight that wane.
We are the bound
sheaves of a meadow stood in waiting.

The curve where the land
and the sky meet
is an arc swept past scope of the mortal.

"Be not afraid," he began,
and kept to the end his message whole
that we will at the end all
whisper as we sway to the quieting note

Of an enveloping hand
sweeping knowingly through the grain—
reaping a yield of man.

# AROUND TROUPSBURG

The night wraps its scarf
of silver-blue gloom around the moon
and trains its face to glow
upon the lonely Amish barn roof
and the silent silo.

The merciful day
drapes its yellow throw
from hill to hill
across the husky rolling shoulders
of the horizon.

Little wonder the caretakers
of hoe and horse plow hold with a will
greater than their own—
its infinite tenderness and pity;
its correction.

They give thanks at noon
for a biblical bounty beneath the sun.
At night they pray
for rainfall upon the dry stacked stone
in the hollows of the city.

# WATCHING AMISH FARMERS

Heal their hands who bring forth fruit.
Wash and anoint with nard their feet
from enamel basin and alabaster box.

Dry their toes with corn silk
and reliquary their sacrificial socks.
Bathe their debtors in milk and honey.

They have no use for tie with suit.
They are of dusty broadfall trouser ilk.
Cities they find fetid.

One owns but is not owned by money.
The sun gilds their paired Belgians,
granary, and chin and hay-field stubble.

They motion roadside and beg us eat.
Their silos house anti-rations.
Their eyes command all hunger hatred.

Keep whole their lands wholly resolute
with covenants of hollyhocks—
with humilities that escape the nations.

# FIELD HANDS

A single bead of sweat descends
my brother's brow
under the sun in a field
where we are lifting hay bales
into a lumbering cart.

*Straw*, I think to myself,
*for making Pharaoh's bricks.*
Fifty years on,
I would catch that imperial bead
in a golden cup

And render of it a sacred oil
to anoint his head
transformative of his social status.
He will be foreman now
of the walls and the monoliths

And of all the great works.
His cart will be a chariot.
He will wear onyx and pearl.
He will dream he is floating
on the starlit sable water of the Nile.

# TOUR OF THE BIG APPLE

The ships and the sailing craft are magnificent in the harbor.
The skyline is astonishing.
The magnitude of the place defies comprehension—
the culture, the transnationality,
the food readily made resident here from all over the world,

Music, theater, dance, television, glamor,
Times Square and the flashing lights of Broadway.
It is the modern Constantinople, the seat
of fashion, art, medicine, learning, experiment, knowledge
of all things of which knowledge may be gained.

And here, my friends, our tour begins.
This, ladies and gentlemen, is a destitute American male
of roughly fifty years of age—
dressed in a rancid raincoat and tattered pants and grubby shirt
and otherwise clad except for his squalid feet.

He is sleeping for want of warmth atop a steam grate
not far from Radio City Music Hall, where you will soon be
treated to a dazzling performance.
This man must expect to be handled like a listless side of beef.
After all, must not the glitz grill its meat?

# VESPER

The downy snow along a limb
and this frizz
of limbs
against disarming winter air
are not a curling-powder hurled

Hollow-point—
not nubby grip a pistol knows.
Among our bramble of hymns
his hymn
would pepper those crows

With a scattershot care.
The grim
of killers we anoint
holds a 6:00 p.m. audience edge.
His noel—It quickens. It goes.

A jot. A flair.
A trigger trilling in a hedge.
A vesper sparrow there
with claw so naturally knurled—
the peaceable kingdom is his.

# THE FENCE LINE

The Z-pattern split-rail fence argues its zigzag way
up the hillside and over the crest
    as if it would like leave to wander into the sky.

And we who change direction aimlessly, do we lay
claim to the right to determine paths of perfection
    with borders that serve mere utility?

The mind maps those extents that serve best
these dramatic and frequent turns of earthly bounds.
    The heart supplies the meaning of connection.

The circumference of the gaze in the all-seeing eye
of compassion sets its markers about all grounds—
    or fences and men would ever encompass futility.

# SONNET FOR A PRIMAL WOOD

This is the light and these the leaves despair
had been had Adam woke to no one there.
Little has changed in this garden since that.
We inhabit this lonely cage of bones
dug from clay and set upon Ararat
to teach the earth the meaning of its stones.
We are not dense core but the tender air
brought forth through the ages from the forest
that traces to the tree of Eve's great dare.
Our flesh, however pure, will not have rest
in this paradise of impermanence
that pins a leaf against the clothes we wear.
We can but show such debt due deference
and work to earn a world our sires thought flat.

# LET THESE CONSECRATE MAY

Every rank and stripe of seed sees
to it that its army overwhelms
the no-man's-land of the landscape.

It is a shrapnel merciless
against wide-brim straw sun helms
        and mouths agape.

We have no answer to parachutes—
no chevaux-de-frise
to waylay the wave of raw recruits

Before they reach our shirtsleeves,
where like paratroopers on D-day
        they overrun our safe suits.

If this is the enemy, no one grieves
arms laid down in the grass.
Let these projectiles consecrate May.

Surrender means that defeat yields
only natural harms in minefields
        of horehound and sassafras.

# THREE APPLE TREES SEEN AS IF CAST IN BRONZE

*For Leland, Michael, and Thomas*

Three gnarled trees twisted with year
and water and light,
with shifting soil and with contorted

Root and wind, stand hunched
such that each uses the space
and attitude afforded him by another.

One moans in the bitterness of winter.
One welcomes the snowflakes
upon his head. One is indifferent.

So long have they held their
respective positions in this collective
need that one has come to brace

The lower back of the one who in turn
steadies the knees of the one who
faces the wind for them all.

# BURDOCK

Let the burdock go.
Let it be
at my elbow.
Let it make something like a bouquet
of bristles on my woolen cap.

In fact, let it consume
my worst desires
still clinging until
I am wearing it
to the extremities of shirt and trousers.

Those we picked at end of day
from socks and scarves
tossed to the fires
of more than fifty years ago—
make one day a cairn of them above me.

# I DREAMT OF FAWNS

Nature's creator stepped
mercifully into the meadow—
a flowering field
of tranquility set in the seed.
And the sun leapt

Where cumulus collected
in placid pool revealed—
and the wild weed
withered and went below,
and a doe and her two dead

Fawns were reunited,
and every stag
and every worshipped
and war-borne faltering flag
genuflected.

## A SUPPLICATION

I came from the fire-
escape above your head.
I came from the gutter.
I came from my bed
a bench and from alley.
I came from your cellar

And your family tree.
I came from nowhere.
I came from every-

where. Just a little
water, a cover to undo
the wind, my brother.
I pray you. I pray you.
I have one more degree
to make it through.

It was a cold winter.
I have one more mile
to go. Just a morsel,

Mind you, a handful,
half a smile, a patch for
my shirt, a bubble-
gum plug for the hole
in my shoe, sweet sister.
I pray you. I pray you.

# A DISTANT WOOD

I've been making for a distant wood
an image in my mind
of a sky with light and leaves—
of some gentle good.
I've decided to leave behind
sooty memories of brickbat and glass
for bluebell sleeves
and streams that singing pass

Unsullied by city sirens. I have sought
among sour voices a sylvan choir
that sings of brotherhood
to an embittered humankind.
I'm shunning what was never mine
for wild rye and woodbine
and the downy offerings of a thought
that knows no thorn, no barbed wire.

I'm preparing to be taking only what
I need to keep my bones
wound with muscle and blood
and in my skin kept whole.
I've been making for a distant wood
wherein to rest my soul.
I'm looking to find behind hard stones
a gentle wind and grass.

# SAGUARO

These observing silence
in the sunlight of searing hours
and wind-freeze of nights

Raise their arms tirelessly,
like Stonehenge ancients
in praise of quasar and moon:

Druids of green orders
whose staves we appropriate
to walk with here in the sun—

Performing their rites
with a devotion we
might come to appreciate

When after three hundred years
our souls are cosmic lights
and their ribs the ribs of men.

# WIND IN A WOOD

I bid you enter with me—
I avail

The sourwood,
the bitter-leaving trees—

And attest
these spirits pure at root.

With me journey,
human frail,

Into mortal forest
of buried beauties—

Of hidden good
and of unblemished fruit.

# GIRL WITH MILKWEED

She runs the playground
grinning with the milky seed streaming
behind from the burst green bag.
What does she know
of the chances that rise and fall—
that float in limbo
awhile and then land scattershot around?

This is fairy dust teasing the screaming
fulcrum of the teeter-totter.
This is pixie glitter
in the long chains of the swing set.
It is a message from her God
to follow grace and shun fate and a fool—
to think without forgetting to feel.

Her teachers would gag
to read the hopeless writing on the wall
that surrounds the school.
It is a good bet or better
she will not forget
her lessons on which wonders prove real
between earthly and supernal pod.

# BALL GONE ASTRAY

Child, I might well tell you
nothing rolls here
crooked upon the earth—

But I'd as surely in the end
hand you a leaf of truth
that might survive the year.

And I might say to you
that all of this turns to bliss
and love and faith—

That the leaves beneath
which you run will descend
to a faultless ball;

That your several destinies
will make a roll call
of the utterly blameless—

But I must return to you
this smoothly perfect sphere
of yours in lieu of these.

# ASPENS REFLECTED ON WATER

Stoic now, I keep coming back here to listen to the rills
of this antediluvian waterway
to try to discern
the preposterous works of fiction

In the scandalous chronicles of history.
Our unlettered ancestors also once interpreted
these leaves that curl on the limbs of trees and crumble
like Dead Sea scrolls.

They prattle out the tickertapes of vaunted disquisition.
But all I can hear is the trickle
of futility,
and all I can see is nature's unaccountable scrawl

In an exotic cuneiform vetted
upon this liquid parchment scrolling by—
eyeing the warped reflection of I don't know how many
crooked pencils.

# RETREAT FOR AN AMPUTEE

Here she advances remote from tripwire
to claymore.
Here no
question of posttraumatic

Stress disorder
offends the status quo;
no nubile nurse or orderly salutes cutely.
There's just

Allegheny splendor
and the quietude of the mutely
dramatic.
Why her? Why not? It's all a bust;

Then echo—
sent on and on from the leg's latent fire—
reacquires its faith in acoustic
shadow.

# THE FALL

A leaf,
like a false apple
blossom, does not
do very much

At all to address
original sin
or the existential
questions of

The examined
life except to taste
the rain
and imbibe the sky

And feel
the bitter wind
and the heavy hail
and welcome

The sun awhile
and die
and fall away. I
rake up many lives.

# MISSIVE FOR THE REALTOR

I require, dear realtor, a yard with a weeping willow
and the scent of cut grass.
When I go up the stairs

I want there to be
a landing with a round cupola with windows round
overlooking the lawn.

There I will make my brown study
looking out upon the willow.
There I will plead for the grass

Until the leaves all
turn brown and turn and gracefully forgive the wind
and the ground.

I want a house with an old stone wall
I can let go with all that has gone
to rockfoil and ivy—

To indolent rains fallen upon its lichen-hosted moss—
when I go up the stairs
to turn toward a room I do not know.

# COIN FOR A FRIEND, VIOLATED

Were it thinkable in the range
of adventure to be seduced,
ultimately, by forced failure,
she well might in the ceaseless exchange
and rape of shell find rest.

But she is not slave by sailor
to be broken—
not now compelled, though reduced
at the end to the tossing of a token
to the surface.

Were all by time impressed,
still their indenture could not delay
bad-breathed heathen.
Neither might violent particulars impede
her windward toward Elysian isles.

For this, through dire need
and the debt her passage compiles,
she must guard a luck-piece
got of tide and trust to throw her one day
at the sea in jest.

# AN OLD SOUTHERNER
# RESPONDS TO A TRAIN

*For Sterling A. Brown*

Ol' blue train,
why you moan?
Got you resentment?
Be yo' luva o' chil' gone?

Weight o' da black
stone 'long yo' spine
got you down?
Confine o' da fire

In yo' gut and da tie an' track,
s' narra an' s' unkin',
got you low?
Ol' blue train,

Soun' you make
be da pullin' o' contentment—
*eva s' slow*—
'gainst yo' desire.

# SPIDERS' THREADS

Carefully before dawn,
these tenderly minded threads were strung
from grass blade to tree-shaded or sunburned blade of grass.

Delicately, deftly done,
the spinning of spiders asks why humanity runs
thoughtlessly, carelessly, oblivious to every subtle warning.

All duties become crass,
and so many fine distinctions have gone
that once lent an enlightened elegance to our garish adorning.

But then time is hung
in the fey raiment of intentions that pass
with daylight and go forgotten into the filaments of the sun.

The elm this morning
sways as if weaving a spell over the lawn
that no insensible step should sever our tenuous connections.

# SELECTIVE MEMORY

This is her garden,
these her flowers,
her winters number nearly ninety among.
She'd not have heeded thief of Eden.

Petals dance
and stars bloom
where she moves
beneath a passion of Earth's new moon.

And this is her groom—
bud-bursting fig tree that has sung
of beautiful loves,
and had kept the sudden

Rude showers
at a distance,
and was no wretched man-rib flung,
and dared never attempt its kiss too soon.

# JOHN CONRAD

John Conrad dug ditches
and grew his garden
    and gave away his money

And his time
and his cabbages
and just about everything else

He did or did not have. John C.
suffered in silence
    the world-ending cruelties

Of the avaricious.
And then he died
with another bushel in his arms

And a world on his shoulders—
and thus to John Conrad
    collected all of these riches.

# SUBURBAN RITUAL

In his ox-blood size-eleven
slippers over white tube socks
and over his plaid
    pajamas a terry-cloth

Robe, Mr. Adam McNair
comes from louvered
sunscreen sliding plate-glass
    door early over grass

Blades clipped as putting pad
to a silver mailbox
where are delivered
    bills and letters to 777

Mercy Square Lane, "Nauth,"
Enchanting Meadows, Mass.—
his aimless hair
    Hoovered toward heaven.

## MOONLIT PRIVATE DRIVE

A charwoman reserved for eons arrived
among the flung-vase shard-spray
of stars has passed eternities on her way
to work through the frozen-out spaces

Between the gunnysack dying comets
of her kind and a vibrant star
of the constellation where she has come
to dust this Chippendale home of a world—

To make right the overturned chair
and to hide the wrong-color hair upon
a pillow. She arrives on a normal
sort of day, soaking up their spilled milk,

Sweeping, cleaning the cigar-smoke-
begrimed superior-crystal dome
of the mantel clock, wiping lipstick from
a wine glass quickly so as to be mopping

Up her mistress's tears from the writhing
drive's pooled pavement. She
empties the dust bin of history. She
shakes out her rags of filth and disillusion.

# THE MARTYRS

Icicles line the eaves and the peaks
down along both sides of Green Street.
Are they spears? Arrows?
Should we think of Saint Sebastian?
Of a winter afternoon
even a sickly sun will beat
down strong enough upon an armory

To melt its pointed throws.
Or are these martyrs lined for view
down along a human history
of endless war and peacetime dividend?
We've not been quite certain
since the season began.
Warmer weather will be here soon.

In fact, in a matter of mere weeks—
and it won't matter what we do
with symbols. Armaments, perhaps.
But, as if they cared for man
and humanity's fate, tears descend
their long, gaunt cheeks
and settle into melting snowmen's caps.

## ALL MY BONES

All my bones shall say
what weight remained
with sinew stripped
from the body's chain.

All my blood shall count
the beating gained
when death has clipped
life's vacant vein.

All my breath shall tell
a greater mount
than earth can gain.
What does love weigh?

All winds shall swell
to raise this clay
made ashes whipped
where flesh lay chained.

# MICHELANGELO

The world does
not care
what lies along the edge
of the chisel or
upon the face

Of the hammer.
It sees only David there.
Before he was
were hunger, privilege,
envy, apathy, aggression—

Beggar, disgrace,
lunatic, whore,
putrid cart of fishmonger.
Each a model for
his perfection.

# GRANITE PROCLAMATIONS

The soil upon one grave is newly compacted.
Lifeless leaves are blown across it like loose roof shingles.
All of the markers wearily attest the dead
at awkward, misanthropic angles.

The derelict headstone has yet to be placed.
He lies here beneath a lid within walls of missing windows.
From his body all has been exacted.
The skeletal limbs of trees motion to the wind

To fade these names with blowing snows.
What we say we are, time and truth rescind.
Even one's granite-chiseled proclamations are soon erased.
A solemn woman plants her plastic flowers

As if they might shame a groundskeeper's sense of finality.
She wanders a habitation of absent-minded hours—
reading on a lightless inner eyelid a gray banality:
*All monuments to man's empty structures are soon defaced.*

# LEAF AND AFTERLIFE

And then a leaf fell
    to earth
where I went today
    with an expansive view

    Among the trees.
I was the sole
one there
    to see it fall.

Thus it must be somewhere
    it is true
among the all
    that the soul of a single

    Leaf had birth
where all confine falls away
and all is new
    where no one sees.

# WINTER DEPTHS

Most of an afternoon
I have been content to have been
sitting here
sorting out a black tangle of branches

Scratching at the roof;
listening to the wind berate
the shingles
and the eaves—

Recalling a love enwound
in the long dark locks of self-reproach
that shake out their brittle ice
and leaves.

# FOUNTAINHEAD

Ms. Jane Pittman,
created of one man's brains,
drank of that forbidden

Fountain and
the whole ocean,
Mr. Ernest J. Gaines,

Started in
to thirst for the hidden
waters of the promised land.

# PALM READING

In this right hand what is writ that removes the mask
from features that sought a path of vanity or cut
off the mis-sojourned goes midcourse?
And what is this line that calms no argument among

These major themes of body, heart, and head?
And what are these that cross neither parallel nor
perpendicular to one another the central artery there?

I try to interpret my chosen ways, but it all ends
in nothing much to say about the schism at most atlas
seams connecting alley-chasm and thoroughfare.
I conclude a hand has lines on it that map the plans

One's steps erase. So in this left hand what is read
but the aging of two palms that grasped as child
a common clay and shaped that they might find His face.

# ABOUT THE AUTHOR

A professional editor and writer, DARIL BENTLEY studied with poet and Creative Writing Program founder Milton Kessler at Binghamton University. He is author of several volumes of poetry and is author/editor of *The Bentley Guide to Poets & Poetry in English: Chaucer to Brodsky.*

Mr. Bentley has been called "the male Mary Oliver" for his nature poetry, his work also compared favorably with the poetry of naturalist poets Robert Frost and Norwegian Rolf Jacobsen. However, his subject matter (infused everywhere with moral and spiritual import) is diverse and eclectic. In fact, he refers to his poetry as New Eclecticism.

He has been a semifinalist for the Yale Series of Younger Poets Award, a finalist for the New Mexico Book Award for Poetry, and is recipient of an Honorable Mention in the Writer's Digest International Book Award for Self-published Poetry. He has been published in numerous poetry journals in the U.S. and abroad and is a Black Mountain Press *The 64 Best Poets* series author.

He is active in community volunteer work and is founder of POST (Poetry Outreach of the Southern Tier) and PARS (Poets of the Area Reading Series) in the Southern Tier region of New York State, where he makes his home in Elmira, NY, with the love of his life Cilisa.

www.ingramcontent.com/pod-product-compliance
Lightning Source LLC
LaVergne TN
LVHW051703080426
835511LV00017B/2704